# Decorating Baskets

*by Dawn Cusick*

A Sterling/**Lark** book

Sterling Publishing Co., Inc., New York

# Decorating Baskets

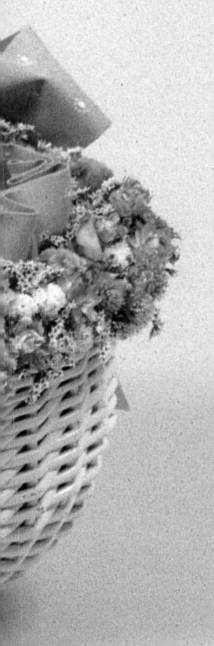

Published in 1990 by Sterling Publishing Co., Inc.
387 Park Avenue South, New York, NY 10016

© 1990 Altamont Press

A Sterling/Lark Book

Produced by Altamont Press
50 College Street, Asheville, NC 28801, USA

Photography: Evan Bracken
Typesetting: Val Ward, Elaine Thompson
Design and Production: Judy Clark
Special Assistance: Newton Smith

Special thanks to Julianne Bronder for her enthusiasm
and technical assistance. .

Library of Congress Cataloging-in-Publication Data
    Decorating baskets / by Dawn Cusick.
        p.        cm.
    "A Sterling/Lark Book."
    Includes bibliographical references.
    ISBN 0-8069-5824-3
    1. Basket making.      I. Title
    TT879.B3C87      1989
    746.41'2 -- dc20
                                            89-21903
                                            CIP


ISBN 0-8069-5824-3

Distributed in Canada by Sterling Publishing Company,
c/o Canadian Manda Group, P.O. Box 920, Station U,
Toronto, Ontario   M8Z 5P9, Canada

Printed in Hong Kong

# Contents

# Introduction

## Baskets Through History

The fibers of basketry's history are intricately woven through many cultures, on every continent, over thousands of years. Primitive baskets can be traced back as far as the Stone Age, when people migrated frequently in search of new food sources. These first baskets were used to transport excess food and fire supplies (which previously had been left to rot), and represent one of man's first successful attempts to manipulate the natural resources of his environment. Twigs and branches were soon woven together to form fishing baskets, and

these same weaving techniques and materials were used to produce floor mats, sandals, water jugs, molds for pottery, Egyptian chariots, and even South African Zulu huts.

Baskets were the perfect solution to early man's need for luggage because their materials were plentiful and lightweight, but the popularity of baskets did not decline after more modern forms of luggage were invented. The shapes and styles of these baskets, however, became more customized to the personalities and lifestyles of various cultures.

In the early 1900s, as the

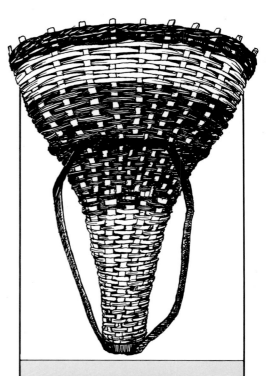

**Choctaw Indian Baskets**

*Baskets made by the Choctaw Indians of Louisiana were used to carry harvested grains and produce in from the fields. They were made primarily from split cane.*

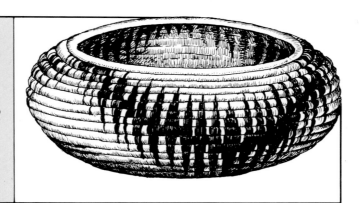

**Pomo Indian Baskets**

*Favorites of museums and collectors, Pomo Indian baskets represent a tradition of basketmaking in Northern California that dates back more than 3,500 years. In the 1800s, most of their baskets were woven and used for carrying food. In the 1900s, though, outsiders began requesting decorative coiled baskets in large numbers.*

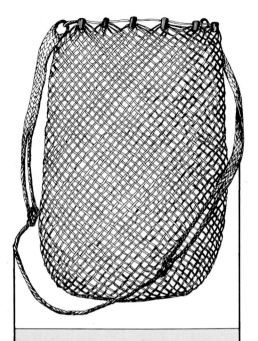

**Mission Indian Baskets**

*Made primarily from bast fibers, baskets made by the Mission Indians of California often resemble netting. The basket shown here was designed to carry fresh fish home from fishing trips.*

industrial revolution in the United States began to change the financial relationship between human labor and profit margins, many companies stopped producing baskets. Basketmaking professionals soon became unemployed, eventually dying off without training new apprentices in the craft. Non-industrialized nations with an abundance of cheap labor and raw materials became the world's leading producers of baskets. It's interesting to note that a successful basketmaking machine has never been invented — all baskets are still made by hand.

When fiber artists became intrigued in the '60s with the aesthetic potential of basketry, they were confronted with a serious void of experienced teachers. Learning the craft through trial-and-error methods, however, produced a new dimension to basketry, and few of today's basketmakers consider themselves limited to traditional shapes or materials. Glass, bark, paper, and other unusual fibers have all been woven into baskets.

**Appalalachian Mountain Baskets**

*Settlers from England, Scotland, and Germany brought their home basketmaking traditions with them to these remote mountains in the 1800s. The baskets were woven with willow, hickory, white oak, and ash, and were used to raise bread dough in, as beehives, and to gather eggs.*

# Decorating Baskets

Basketry is also experiencing a surge of new popularity from crafters, who see the potential of making baskets functional once again. Their styles and shapes can be embellished and customized to decorate any location in the home, or they can be used as the cave men used them, as holding vessels for cherished items.

When you go shopping for baskets to make some of the projects in this book, you may be surprised at the tremendous variety of sizes and shapes available. You may also be surprised to find them inexpensively priced. Five-and-dime and variety stores are usually cheaper than department stores, where the addition of a coat of paint or varnish often triples the price.

**Charleston Sweet Grass Baskets**

*Also known as Low Country, Gullah, Afro-American, Coiled, Sweet Grass, Sea Grass, and Mount Pleasant baskets, these baskets are made in Charleston, South Carolina, in the tradition of African basketmaking. The basketmakers bind fine sweet grass with strips of pal-etto and weave them into coiled baskets.*

Other items for decorating baskets are equally inexpensive. Spanish moss, for example, which is used to cover floral foam and form rim bases, is usually available for just a few dollars a bag . . . and one bag can decorate a lot of baskets! Once your imagination gets going, you may find a treasure of basket decorating items in your own home.

Remember that collection of miniature pine cones or seashells you collected on vacation three years ago? It just might make a gorgeous basket. Open your boxes of Christmas ornaments a week or two early this year and you'll undoubtedly find some items perfect for decorating baskets.

Another fun part of basket decorating is how quickly a project can be completed. Need a centerpiece for a special party tonight? Just borrow some items from your table setting (a wine glass or linen napkin), attach them to a basket with wire or hot glue, form a small bouquet around them with fresh or dried flowers, and garnish with some fruit or vegetables from your dinner menu and you have a perfectly coordinated basket centerpiece. After the party,

**Shaker Baskets**

*Made by the religious Shaker community in New England from the early 1800s through the 1970s, these baskets are well known for their incredible craftsmanship. (The Shakers believed in heaven on earth, and wanted their work to last a thousand years.) Although rarely decorative, the symmetry and fine materials (hickory, ash, oak, and poplar) in these baskets have made them popular since their first appearance.*

the basket can be disassembled; areas with glue spots can be covered with fabric or moss when you make a new decorated basket.

You'll find that decorating baskets encompasses a wide range of styles — everything from the ultra formal to baskets made for pure fun. Antique lovers are becoming fascinated with the idea of decorating the older baskets they've been cherishing for years.

Because there's always the chance your antique basket may hold a special place in the history of basketry, avoid using hot glue directly on the basket. Instead, as basket designer and antique dealer Ron Clemmer recommends, form your decorated arrangements on your work table,

using hot glue as needed. Then wire your arrangement to the basket. Later, if you decide to re-design the basket, you can remove the wired bouquet without causing damage.

Julianne Bronder, a floral designer whose clientele enjoys the popular country look, began decorating baskets after she went searching for natural decorating materials to complement her fresh and dried flowers. Since most baskets are made of natural materials — willow, oak, mountain ash, bamboo, birch, and vine, just to name a few — they were just what she was looking for. Julie notes that many of her most successful decorated baskets were the result of looking at a basket from all angles. "I like to turn a

**Philippine Island Baskets**

*Baskets from the Philippine Islands are known for both their practicality and their beauty. The basket shown here is made from varying widths of split bamboo and is used to carry living poultry.*

basket upside down, on its side, hang it on a wall, imagine it without a handle, or even consider moving the handle to another place on the basket before I begin to decorate."

We hope this book will inspire you to decorate your home and surprise your friends with unique baskets. We also hope the variety of designs and shapes presented in this book will enhance your appreciation for the potential that all baskets hold.

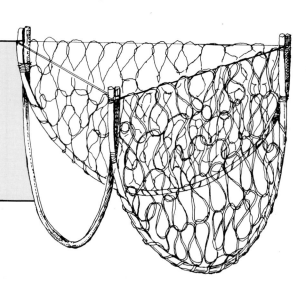

**Baskets as Art**

*Since the early '60s, artists have been exploring new shapes and materials in basketry, stretching the boundaries of what defines a basket.*
*Basket by Joanne Segal Bradford, 1986; rattan, dye, knotless netting; 22½ by 19 by 17 inches.*

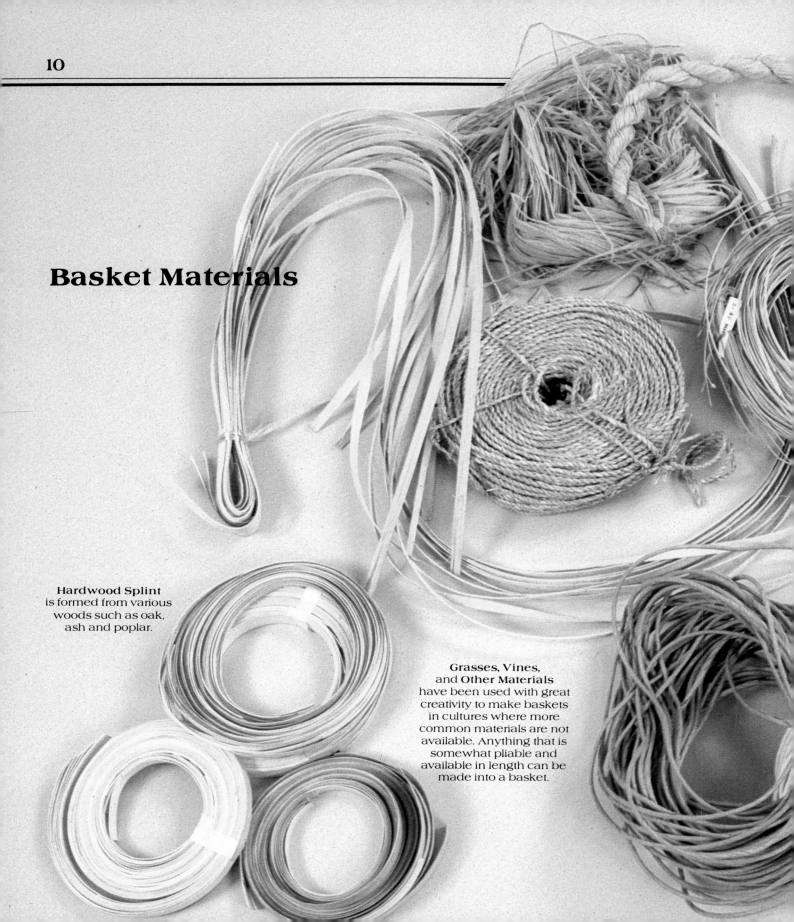

# Basket Materials

**Hardwood Splint** is formed from various woods such as oak, ash and poplar.

**Grasses, Vines, and Other Materials** have been used with great creativity to make baskets in cultures where more common materials are not available. Anything that is somewhat pliable and available in length can be made into a basket.

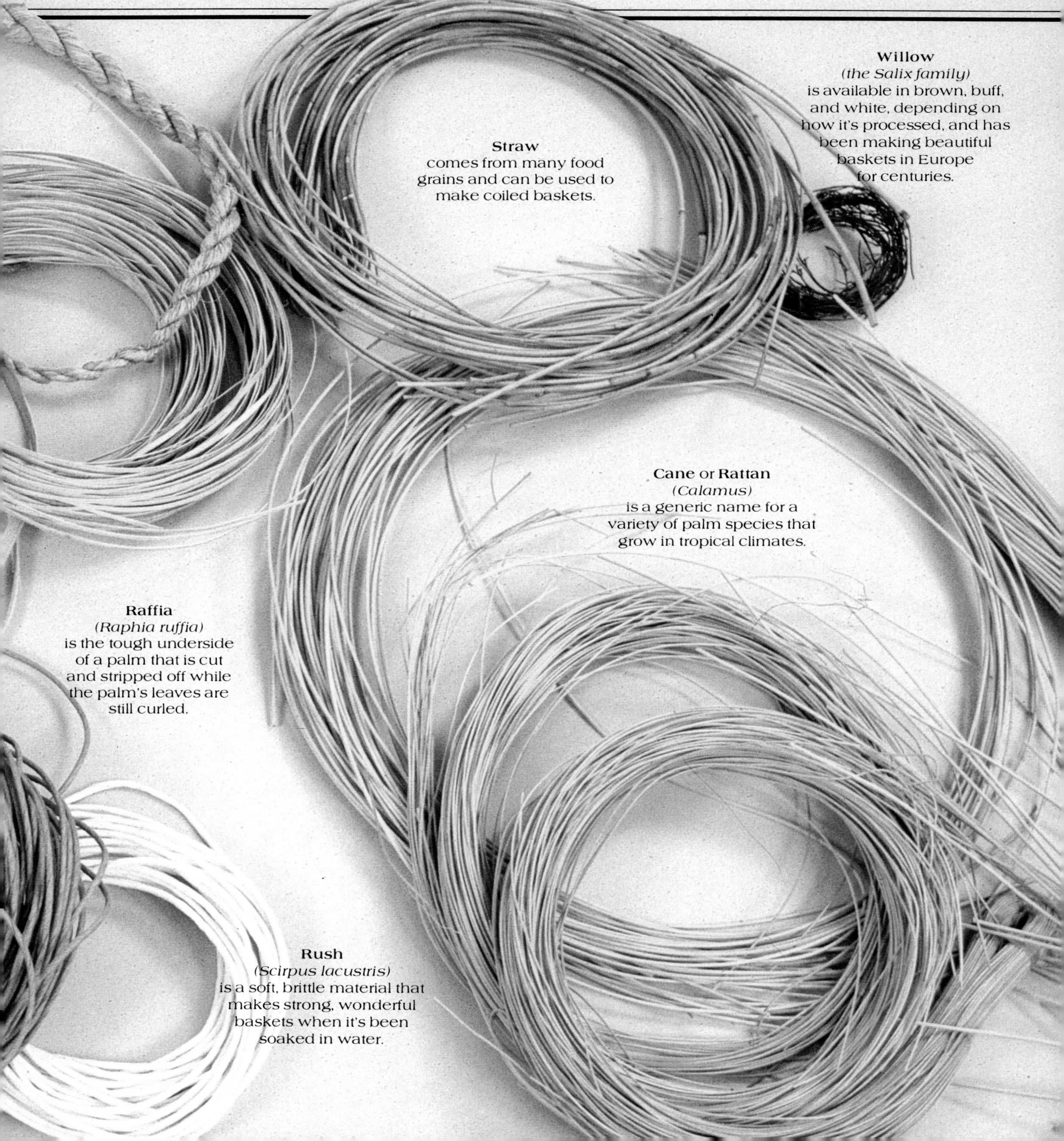

**Willow**
*(the Salix family)*
is available in brown, buff,
and white, depending on
how it's processed, and has
been making beautiful
baskets in Europe
for centuries.

**Straw**
comes from many food
grains and can be used to
make coiled baskets.

**Cane** or **Rattan**
*(Calamus)*
is a generic name for a
variety of palm species that
grow in tropical climates.

**Raffia**
*(Raphia ruffia)*
is the tough underside
of a palm that is cut
and stripped off while
the palm's leaves are
still curled.

**Rush**
*(Scirpus lacustris)*
is a soft, brittle material that
makes strong, wonderful
baskets when it's been
soaked in water.

# How Baskets Are Made

There are several steps to basketmaking that are universal to all basketmakers. They include: sorting lengths and thicknesses of the basket material for different parts of the basket; identifying the "wrong" side (the side that splinters when bent) of the material; and soaking stiff materials in water to increase pliability. From here basketmakers branch off into different methods, dictated by their individual preferences and the materials available to them.

The **Plaiting** method of making baskets is popular with beginners because the warp and weft materials are the same and therefore interchangeable. Geometric designs can be created in the basket by rearranging warp and weft strands.

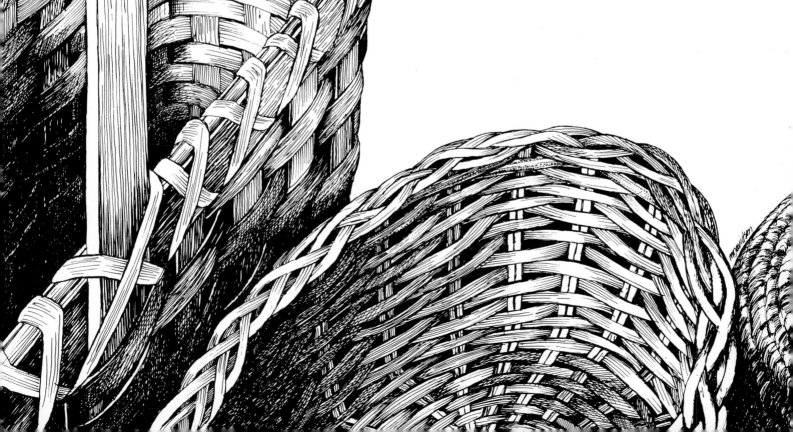

In **Plain Weaving,** upright stakes make up the warp, and the pieces woven around them make up the weft. Because the warp stakes are so much stiffer than the weft materials, a much different appearance is created than with the plaiting method.

**Twining** is a type of plain weaving that uses a weft with two working ends. Twining often produces baskets with texture and is popular with Indian cultures.

**Coiling** works with sewing techniques, instead of weaving, although it's still considered basketry. Rows of coils are stitched together with yarns or other materials. Many Indian tribes are known throughout the world for their high-quality coiled baskets.

# Ideas & Inspiration

After you've practiced the decorating techniques explained in this chapter and made some of your favorite baskets from the chapters that follow, you may want to begin designing your own decorated baskets.

Where do you begin? Since staring at a bare basket for inspiration often has the opposite effect, try starting with something tangible, such as a bouquet of dried or silk flowers, a pair of lovebirds, or a stream of ribbon you find irresistible.

Shop craft supply and novelty stores for anything that catches your eye, and then look for items whose colors are complementary.

Shown below are examples of the variety of items available that can easily spur your imagination. Many come pre-wired for easy attachment to basket rims and handles. Innovative craft novelties, such as artificial mushrooms and flower bulbs, are also available, so don't limit your decorating to traditional materials.

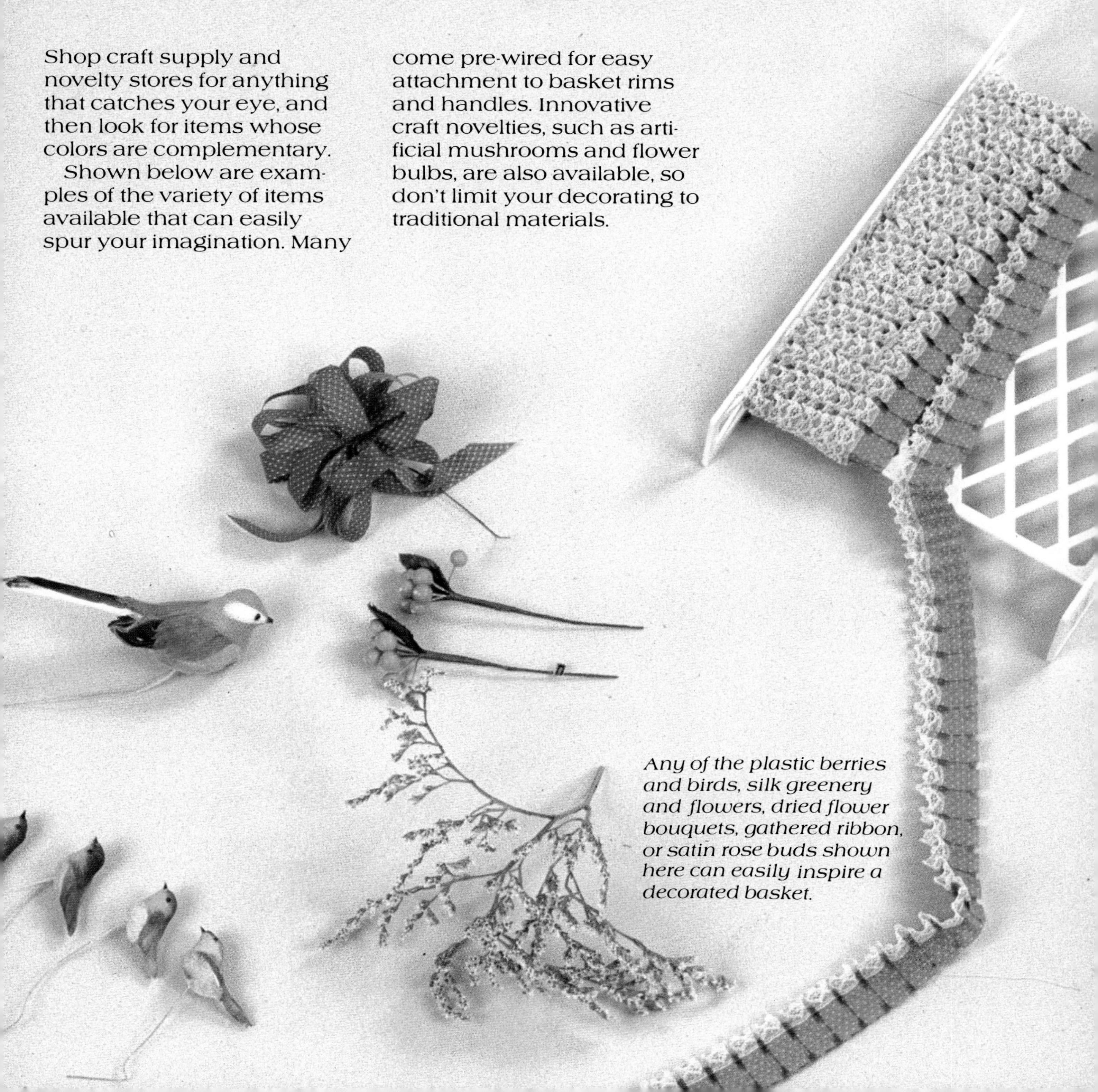

*Any of the plastic berries and birds, silk greenery and flowers, dried flower bouquets, gathered ribbon, or satin rose buds shown here can easily inspire a decorated basket.*

# Tools of the Trade

## Decorating with Floral Materials

**Floral Foam, Pins, and Mosses**

Many of the materials used by floral designers are integral tools for basket decorators. A small block of floral foam hot-glued inside a basket offers immeasurable possibilities. Sprigs of silk, paper, or dried flowers anchor easily into the foam to make bouquets. Or use the foam as a prop for craft novelties such as teddy bears, ducks, or anything else your imagination envisions. To prevent bare, unattractive foam from showing inside your basket, always cover the foam with moss. Floral pins attach the moss to the foam quickly and can be removed later if you decide to re-design the basket.

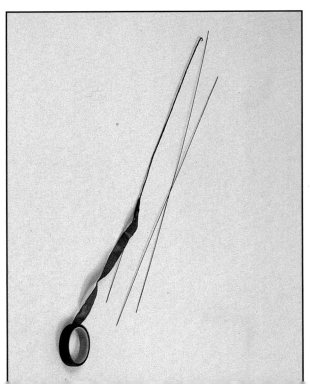

**Floral Wire and Tape**

Another technique borrowed from floral designers is wiring. Simply slip a length of floral wire around an unobtrusive area of the item you wish to attach and twist the wires together to tighten. Then attach the wired item to your basket in the same way. If you were wiring a teddy bear, for instance, an ideal place to attach the wire could be around the bear's neck, since a colorful ribbon could be tied around the wire. Basket designers concerned with detail always wrap their wire with floral tape in a color that blends well with their basket before using.

# Decorating with Glue Guns

For most of the projects in this book you'll need a lightweight "mini glue gun," usually available for under ten dollars in craft supply stores. More expensive models offer the convenience of an upright stand and the capacity to hold more glue. While many experienced crafters find themselves intimidated by glue guns, it usually takes only a few minutes with a glue gun to feel like a pro.

The adhesive glue used in glue guns is far stronger than the liquid glues used by school children, and you may be surprised at the wide range of items that can be hot-glued. Fabric, ribbon, mosses, dried flowers, fruits, nuts, and decorative novelties can all be securely attached to a basket with hot glue.

**Working Tips:**
• While your glue gun is heating up, spread a protective layer of newspaper over your work area. If your glue gun does not have a stand, find a glass plate or other non-flammable item to rest it on.
• Hold larger items in place for at least a minute after gluing to ensure proper bonding. Extremely large or heavy items may need to be attached with wire and then hot-glued for reinforcement. It is often helpful to place

these larger items first, and then glue smaller items around them.
• You may notice strands of glue that resemble spider webs on your basket. Don't worry about them as you're working — they'll easily pull off later.

**Safety Tips:**
• If this is your first time working with a glue gun, you may be tempted to touch the glue. Take our word for it: it's hot! Also avoid touching any metal parts of the glue gun.
(A leading manufacturer is test marketing a glue gun in which the glue melts but never gets hot enough

to cause burns. Check your local craft store for availability.)
• Always keep a bowl of ice water near your work area in case of burns.
• Although children may be attracted by their shape and name, glue guns should never be operated by chilren without close adult supervision.
• Always unplug your glue gun as soon as you've finished.

# Decorating with Fabric

## Fabric Stiffening

Available inexpensively in most craft supply stores, fabric stiffeners allow you to decorate baskets with dramatic shapes of fabric, making everything from stand-up bows to actual baskets.

To make the fabric basket shown here, cut a circular piece of fabric with a diameter at least three times the width of the bottom of your mold. (Bathroom trash cans and plant pots make excellent molds.)

Protect your work area with a layer of newspaper and suspend your mold upside down. Now dampen the fabric with water, saturate it with liquid fabric stiffener, and center it over the bottom of the mold. Gather the fabric evenly around the top of the mold. Also dip a piece of cord or string in the stiffener and tie it around the basket in a bow, using a clothespin or other prop to hold the bow in place until dry.

The edges can be hemmed with a sewing machine before stiffening or trimmed with scissors after the fabric has dried. Finally, spray the dried fabric basket with a light layer of copper spray paint.

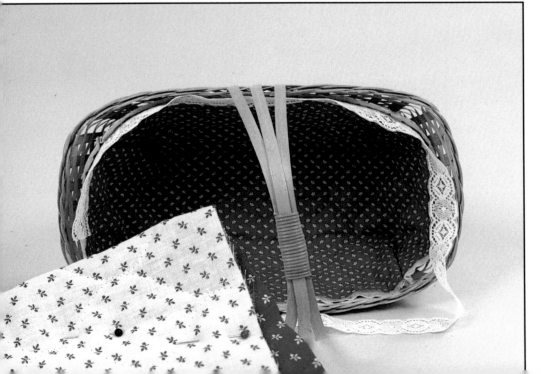

## Linings

There is no exact pattern or formula for making basket linings. Each process is tailored to the unique qualities of the fabric you choose and the individual shape of your basket.

The fabric is fitted to the basket by forming darts in the corners, or by making a series of pleats. With thin fabrics, the darts or pleats can be hot-glued to the basket; with heavier fabrics, such as commercially quilted cottons, the pleats or

## Skirts

Fabric skirts add instant charm and ambiance to any basket. They attach simply to the basket's rim with hot glue and can easily be replaced as the seasons change or you move the basket to a new location.

To make a basket skirt, measure the circumference of your basket's rim and cut a length of fabric about twice as long. Sew side seams together and press. Fold over a top hem and press. Form gathers with loose running stitches or elastic.

Next, sew and press the skirt's bottom hem. If your basket's rim has slopes or curves, you'll need to mark the hem with pins or chalk to ensure evenness. Attach the skirt to the basket's outside rim with hot glue.

Accents of ribbon or lace can be added with a sewing machine or hot glue. Handles can also be embellished with "miniature skirts" using the same techniques.

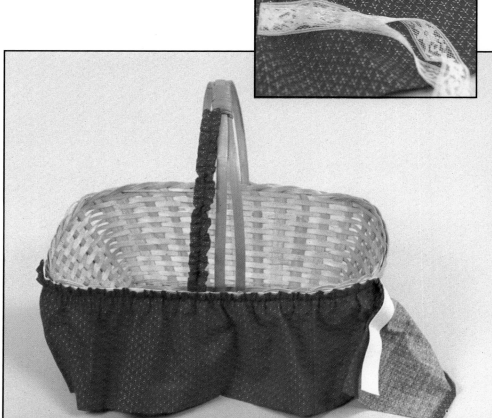

darts should be pinned and sewn before hot-gluing.

Spend some time folding and pleating your fabric into different shapes and positions before plugging in your glue gun.

Other design variations of fabric linings include: adding lace to the top edge of the lining instead of hemming; running a wire or gathering stitches several inches below the lining's top edge for a ruffled effect; or allowing the fabric to drape over the outer edges of the basket.

# Decorating with Ribbon

## Hot-Gluing

Years ago, when the only way to attach ribbon was with a needle and thread, creative decorating with ribbon was out of the question. Today, the miracle of hot glue allows the ribbon to take on a personality of its own.

Begin by playing with the ribbon, twisting and rolling it until you're pleased with the shape it takes. You won't need to glue the entire ribbon — the beginning, the end, and a few strategic places in between is usually enough. Two or three colors of ribbon can also be twisted together and attached.

## Weaving

Any basket with a loose weave can easily be decorated with ribbon. Select a width of ribbon that complements the width of your basket's warp (vertical strips) and its weft (horizontal strips).

Thread one end of the ribbon on a tapestry needle and begin following the weave with your needle from the bottom of the basket up, finishing with both ends of the ribbon on the inside of the basket.

If you have a basket with large warp and weft strips (two or three inches), the ribbon can be woven over and under by hand and then pulled tight until it slips under the weave.

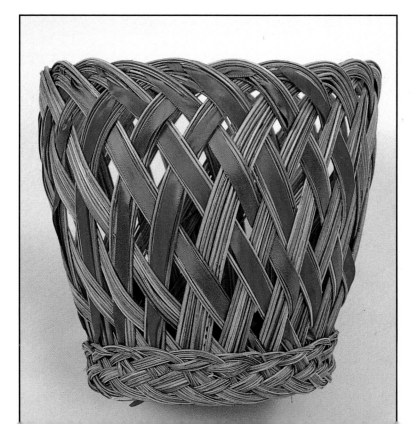

# Decorating with Dried Flowers

Dried flowers make special design accents when glued around basket handles, bows, or craft novelties. They adhere simply and quickly with just a small amount of hot glue, and can be purchased inexpensively or dried fresh from your garden.

Although they appear quite delicate, dried flowers will look beautiful for many years if properly cared for. Some tips to remember:
• a light spray of regular hairspray once a year will help prevent shattering • exposure to direct sunlight will fade the colors of your dried flowers, so avoid displaying them in windows or on tables that receive sunlight • some dried flowers will reabsorb moisture and wilt if exposed to damp areas, so avoid placing them in unventilated bathrooms or near the stove in your kitchen.

## Making Wreath Baskets

When designers recognized the similarity between a wreath base and the circular shape of a basket's rim, a new trend in decorating baskets with dried flowers began.

Since dried flowers do not adhere well to most basketry materials, you'll need to form a base of moss around the rim before beginning. Twist the moss into a tight strip, apply hot glue to the basket's rim, and mold the moss around the rim. (Tip: use a glass jar or other implement to press the moss in place to avoid glue burns.)

For the basket shown here, a stem of German statice is cut into two- to three-inch strips and then glued one at a time into the moss. The statice is placed at an angle and is glued in the same direction all the way around the basket. Begin in the center of the moss and then work the inner and outer edges. After the base of statice is finished, the larger flowers, such as clover, are glued in place. Smaller flowers, such as baby's breath, are always glued in last and are used to cover any imperfections or bare spots.

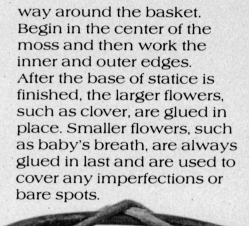

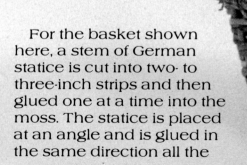

# Surface Design

## Washes and Glazes

Decorating baskets with washes and glazes allows you to create very unique, custom colors. After a base coat of color is applied to the basket, a second coat of diluted paint is applied to enhance the color of the base coat. If this second coat is lighter than the base coat, it's called a wash; if it's darker than the base coat, it's called a glaze.

To create a washed or glazed finish you'll need: an ordinary basket, one can of aerosol sealer (available in hardware or paint stores), one can of aerosol varnish for the finishing coat, one tube of acrylic or oil paint for the base coat, one tube of acrylic or oil paint for the second coat (a tube of black for a glaze; a tube of white for a wash), appropriate thinner or solvent (matte or gloss for acrylic paint, mineral spirits for oil paint), a small brush with natural bristles, one absorbent, lint-free cloth.

*Basket with Peach Glaze*

*Peach Basket with Wash*

Begin with a clean, dry basket. Apply the sealer coat and allow to dry. Next, apply the base coat. While the base coat is drying, use a small jar or bowl to mix together your wash or glaze mixture. (See directions on page 24 for preparation.) Apply your wash or glaze from the inside out, top to bottom.

After a few minutes, use the cloth to gently wipe off the excess paint. Allow the wash or glaze deposits in recessed areas to remain on the basket. When dry, apply a clear coat of aerosol varnish.

*Peach Basket with Contrasting Glaze*

*Peach Basket with Glaze*

## Splattered Finishes

To create a splattered paint finish you'll need: acrylic or oil paint, appropriate thinner or solvent (matte or gloss for acrylics, turpentine or mineral spirits for oils), a drop cloth or newspaper to protect surrounding areas, several stiff, short-bristled brushes (toothbrushes can be substituted), one can of aerosol sealer (available in hardware and paint stores), one can of aerosol varnish, several rags.

Begin by applying a sealer coat to your clean, dry basket. Apply the base coat of paint in the color of your choice. While the base coat is drying, use the appropriate thinner to dilute several colors of paint in small bowls or jars. Dip a short-bristled brush into the paint, and draw your thumb over the bristles to splatter the paint on the basket.

Apply additional splattered colors to build a tone density you like, occasionally splattering some of the base coat's color to provide depth of tone. Try to vary the sizes of your splatters by changing the distance between the splattering brush and the basket. When finished, apply a clear coat of varnish.

## Tips:

• Aerosol spray cans that are nearly empty can produce a splattered effect by lightly depressing the nozzle. Always allow ample ventilation and protective covering.

• Automobile trunk paints sold in aerosol cans also provide an easy, attractive splattered finish.

## Preparing Washes & Glazes

**A Wash Mixture** is made by combining three parts thinner or solvent to one part white paint and one part base color paint.

**A Glaze Mixture** is made by combining three parts thinner to solvent to one part black paint and one part base color paint.

**Thinners and Solvents** are usually available wherever you purchase oil and acrylic paints. Use matte or gloss acrylic medium to thin acrylic paints, and turpentine or mineral spirits to thin oil paints.

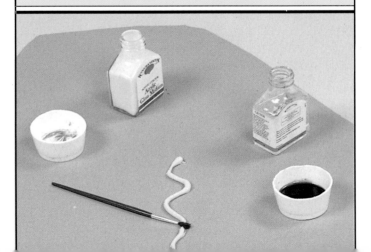

## Wood Staining

Wood stains create natural colors that are easy to apply and blend in with almost every decor.

To create a wood stain finish you'll need: a clean, dry basket, a small can of wood stain, a lint-free cloth, a paint brush, a can of varnish or polyurethane for a clear finish.

Apply the wood stain with a small brush and allow to partially dry. Create a two-tone effect by wiping off any excess stain with a lint-free cloth while allowing the stain to remain in recessed areas. Apply a sealer coat after the stain has dried.

## Wood Stain with Green-Grey Wash

Another popular basket color is achieved by applying a green grey wash over a walnut-colored stain. Choose an oil-based paint for the wash, in a green-grey col-

or several shades lighter than the wood stain. Dilute with thinner (mineral spirits or turpentine) and brush over the dried wood stain. Use a lint-free cloth to gently wipe off any extra wash, allowing the wash to remain in recessed areas. Apply a sealer coat when the wash has dried.

## Metallic Finishes

Metallic finishes add a rustic aura to any basket. Bronzing powders, available in craft supply stores, can be applied to raised areas of the basket's surface for a special glimmering effect.

To create a metallic finish you'll need: one can of spray primer (iron-oxide-red for gold or copper; grey for silver), one can of metallic spray paint, one can of shellac (white for silver; orange for gold or copper), de-natured alcohol for thinning the shellac, one tube of burnt umber oil paint, one can of mineral spirits for oil paint solvent, a soft, lint-free cloth, bronzing powders (gold or silver), bronzng liquid, a soft brush for applying the bronzing powder.

Begin with a clean, dry basket. Prime the basket with a coat of shellac in the appropriate color (white for silver; orange for gold or copper) and allow to dry. Spray on a coat of gold, copper, or silver paint. After the metallic coat of paint has dried, seal with a mixture of two parts de-natured alcohol to one part shellac (orange shellac for gold or copper; white shellac for silver). After the shellac sealer has dried thoroughly, apply a dark glaze made from the burnt umber paint and mineral spirits. When the glaze

is slightly dry, wipe it with a clean, soft, lint-free cloth, allowing the glaze to remain in recessed areas.

Raised areas of the basket can be highlighted with light gold or silver bronzing powder mixed with a small amount of bronzing liquid on the tip of a bristle brush. When the basket is completely dry, apply a clear finish coat.

## Verdigris Green Finish

To create the Verdigris Green Finish shown below, add a copper finish to the basket as described above. Then mix together thalo green, white, and umber oil paint colors in a large bowl and dilute them with mineral spirits. Divide this mixture into three bowls.

Form a dark glazing medium by adding some black oil paint to one of the bowls, and a light glazing medium by adding white oil paint to another of the bowls. The remaining bowl is your medium-tone glazing medium.

Sponge on the darkest color first, then the medium tone, and then the lightest color. Make small runs in the finish by lightly patting the basket with a sponge dipped in mineral spirits.

## Flemish Metallic Finish

A Flemish metallic finish adds a touch of class to ordinary baskets. For best results, choose a base color that's dark, rich, and intense, such as a red, burgundy, dark blue or teal.

To create a Flemish finish you'll need: one can of aerosol sealer (available in hardware and paint stores), acrylic paint (aerosol or tube), one can of aerosol hand cleaner, and one can of aerosol gold, silver or copper metallic paint.

Begin with a clean, dry basket. Apply the sealer coat and allow to dry. Next, apply the base coat. After the base coat has dried, apply another coat of sealer to prevent the spray cleaner from dissolving the base coat.

After this second coat of sealer has dried thoroughly, spray on a heavy coat of cleaner. While the basket is still wet, spray on a light layer of metallic paint. Suspend the basket upside down and allow the paint and cleaner mixture to drip downward.

## Sponged Finish

A sponged finish provides an interesting variety of color tone and texture to a basket.

To create a sponged finish you'll need: one can of aerosol sealer (available in hardware and paint stores), three colors of acrylic paint in tubes (black, white, and a third color of your choice), one bristle brush, several sponges (natural or sea sponge preferred), matte acrylic medium, three small jars, water.

Begin with a clean, dry basket. Apply the sealer coat and allow to dry. In the first bowl, mix together your chosen color with some black paint and dilute it with water and matte acrylic medium. In the second bowl, dilute your chosen color with matte acrylic medium. In the third bowl, mix together your chosen color with some white paint and dilute with water and matte acrylic medium.

Using a bristle brush, apply a coat of the darker paint and allow to dry. Then use a sponge to apply a coat of your chosen color and allow to dry. Then apply light dabs of the lightest color with a sponge. After drying, finish with a clear sealer coat.

## Dyes

Decorating basket surfaces with dye creates deep-toned colors without the splatters and fumes that often accompany other surface design techniques. Always choose a clean wicker basket for your dyeing projects that has not been treated with sealer or varnish.

To create a dyed basket you'll need: a clean wicker basket, dye, a paint brush, varnish or polyurethane for a sealer coat.

Prepare the dye according to package directions. Brush on one to three coats of dye, depending on the intensity of color you like. After the basket is completely dry, apply a sealer coat.

To create a two- or three-tone effect, prepare two colors of dye in separate containers that are larger than the basket's circumference. Dip the basket to the desired level in the lighter color, then turn it upside down and repeat the process in the darker color. The two colors will bleed together in the center.

*Special Occasion*

A *Bon Voyage Gift Basket* makes a special substitute for the traditional traveling gift of a fruit basket. The basket can also be used to present a surprise vacation gift, with a pair of cruise tickets tucked into the beach sand.

Begin by filling an oblong basket with newspaper or straw. Cover this layer with plastic wrap, and spread a thin layer of sand over it to create the beach effect. Then wrap a paper ribbon around the handle, tie a bow off to the side, and attach it with hot glue. Starting at the bow, wrap a stem of silk orchids around the handle. Hot-glue sea shells around the rim, saving a few to tuck into the sand.

Finally, fill the basket with sunglasses, a travel magazine, sun tan oil, and anything else your traveler might enjoy.

This *Victorian Moss and Roses Basket* starts with an ordinary basket that is covered with sheet moss (available in craft supply stores) using a glue gun. The moss is then gently molded to conform to the basket's simple shape. Victorian lace and pearls are draped around the basket and hot-glued in select areas for reinforcement. The silk roses are attached with hot glue. Since the moss is still living, this basket should not be exposed to direct sunlight or it will turn brown.

For the wedding day, fill the basket with rose petals and make a matching tussy mussy to carry as a bouquet or wear as a corsage. (The tussy mussy is made by folding matching roses, pearls, and ribbon up in a handkerchief.)

A *Wedding Day Memory Basket* combines the tradition of something old (a pair of vintage white leather gloves), something new (a string of pearls), something borrowed (a lace handkerchief), and something blue (a garter) into a keepsake center-piece for any room.

The designer began by spraying an old wicker basket with white enamel paint. A length of white net-ting is then tied around the handle and a bow tied into place and hot-glued. White feathers and satin roses are glued into the arrange-ment, with iridescent seed crystals wired on last. The keepsake items are then draped over the edge of the basket.

This *Tulle Wedding Basket* is the perfect centerpiece for a small table at a wedding reception. An ordinary basket is whitewashed and then decorated with a length of lace attached with hot glue. (Lace from the bride's gown, if available, would make a special touch.)

A separate length of lace is then cut into strips and tied together with silver ribbon to make two large bows, allowing enough length in the silver ribbon for streamers. The bows and the lovebirds are then attached to the basket with hot glue. Last, small squares are cut from a yard of white tulle and filled with bird seed, tied with a satin ribbon, and decorated with a satin rose attached with hot glue.

What to give the newlyweds as a wedding gift? . . . a toaster? . . . a silver pie slicer? No way! Surprise them with a *Honeymoon Gift Basket* that's sure to delight.

Begin decorating the basket by wrapping a strip of white netting around the handle, leaving enough netting on each side to tie a bow. Then wrap a length of lavender picot ribbon loosely over the netting and continue wrapping all the way around the handle. Repeat the process with a pale pink satin ribbon, and hot-glue the ribbons at each end of the handle.

Next, hot-glue sprays of silver stars (available in craft supply and novelty stores) into the netting bows, and add pieces of dried German statice and artificial berries to create small bouquets.

The basket is filled with champagne, glasses, fine chocolates, bubble bath, a sea sponge, and fragrant potpourri. Tailor the gifts in the basket you make to the whims and personalities of your newlyweds.

This festive *Happy Birthday Basket* combines birthday gifts and flowers into a decorative arrangement.

A chunk of floral foam is first cut to the shape of the basket and attached with hot glue. Several sprays of silk flowers are inserted into the foam at one end, while a foil-wrapped gift and party trinkets decorate the other end. Streamers of curled ribbon are added last (secured with hot glue) to cover any bare spots.

A two-tone *Mother's Day Basket* is ideal for filling up with special gifts for mom and looks attractive on a bedroom dresser after the holiday passes.

Spray painted first with white enamel, the second color is added to the handle and rim with a small brush and pink acrylic paint. The plant is added next, with Spanish moss tucked around the pot and a bow added for looks.

Fill the remaining space in your basket with the largest gifts first, then tuck smaller items into any bare spots. In the basket shown here, the sachet bag was added first, followed by several Victorian rose candles.

This *Mountain Pounding Basket* reconstructs an old tradition from the Appalachian mountains.

When a new family moved to the area, a pounding basket would be given as a sort of community housewarming gift. Each person brought a pound of something — sugar, butter, nails, flour, etc. — to contribute to the basket and help the new family get started.

The basket shown here is filled first with newspaper and then covered with Spanish moss. The moss shown in this basket was spray painted green before using, but you can leave it natural or choose another color if you like. The paper bow is attached with wire and the basket filled with special items. This basket would make a beautiful showcase for family heirlooms.

This *Welcome-To-The-Neighborhood Basket* makes a thoughtful gift for new neighbors.

The outside of the basket is decorated with small wooden home scenes (available in craft supply and novelty stores) that are attached with hot glue. The basket's handle is decorated with a simple bow made from a strip of measuring tape. The bow is attached with wire so it can be unfolded and put to use by the recipient.

The inside of the basket is lined with a blue denim fabric attached with hot glue. Excelsior makes a decorative filler that is topped with a pair of work gloves, a paint brush, and other useful items for the new home owner. The rosemary plant is a symbolic plant of welcome and adapts well to most climates.

A large, skirted *Victorian Children's Basket* makes a special resting spot for a birthday doll and is a lovely accent to any little girl's room. Underneath and around the doll there is plenty of room to store toys, diapers, baby powders and lotions, etc.

The basket is made by glue-gunning a fabric lining to the basket's inside, and then cutting a length of fabric twice the circumference of the basket for the skirt. The skirt's gathers can be formed with elastic or running stitches. After hemming, the top of the skirt is glue-gunned to the basket's rim, and decorative laces or ribbons can be added if desired. The silk flowers are attached with hot glue.

This *Please-Forgive-Me Basket* makes a special gesture of apology to a loved one.

The handle of the basket is wired with red silk flowers (traditional symbols of passion), and the basket is filled with symbolic gifts. The note card is attached to the bouquet on the handle with matching ribbon.

This vibrant *Party Basket* is perfect for celebrating Mardi Gras, New Year's Eve, Halloween, or other special occasion.

Begin by lining a large basket with quilted metallic fabric (or foil) and hot-gluing in place. Ordinary black and white Halloween masks are then wired to the sides of the basket and decorated with sequins, ribbon, spray glitter, and lengths of gold and silver garland.

The basket can be filled with champagne, snack crackers and cheese, confetti, and small gifts.

# *Scented Baskets*

The mosaic pattern in this *Dried Herb Basket* showcases the beauty of dried herbs and makes a fragrant centerpiece.

Larger items, such as the bay leaves, are wired to the basket, while smaller herbs are attached with hot glue. The basket is decorated in sections, with the pattern outlines applied first and then filled in. The basket's handle is decorated with tightly wrapped red ribbon which is hot-glued at both ends for reinforcement.

The dried herbs include lavender, pearly everlasting, goldenrod, mountain mint, sweet bay leaves, yarrow, anise hyssop, salvia, feverfew, garlic heads, nutmeg, nigella pods, star anise pods, and statice.

This *Fresh Herb Bouquet Basket* is made from flowering herbs and is both beautiful and fragrant.

Begin with a loosely woven basket and a bundle of fresh-picked herbs. Insert the herbs by their stems into the spaces between the basket's warp and weft (vertical and horizontal strips) as your inspiration dictates. Secure them with floral wire, if needed.

The herbs will remain fresh for several days if spritzed with water, and the basket can be filled with plants or gifts.

This *Miniature Victorian Fragrance Basket* attaches to a ceiling fan with clear filament, and can be used instead of a chain to turn the fan on and off.

The basket was first spray painted to match a bedroom decor, and then embellished with everlastings and satin ribbons attached with hot glue. The inside of the basket is filled with a fragrant potpourri, which emits a delicate scent as the basket spins with the blades of the fan.

The herbs include: bay leaves, bee balm, calendula, rosemary, sage, thyme, oregano, anise hyssop, marjoram, and several varieties of mountain mint.

(Tip: If you pick your herbs on a dry afternoon, they will dry naturally on the basket and remain fragrant for months.)

An unusual height and deep colored flowers add an elegant look to this *Potpourri Heart Basket*.

To decorate the basket, first form a base by hot-gluing tightly twisted Spanish moss to the rim. The dried flowers are attached by dabbing hot glue on their stems and inserting them into the moss.

The dried flowers include: blue bachelor buttons and blue delphinium dried in silica gel. The small bouquet at the center of the heart is made with pearly everlasting, blue salvia, and grey dusty miller.

When you've finished decorating, line the bottom of the basket with tissue paper or moss, and fill the basket with wood-chip potpourri. Tip: while floral-petal potpourri is just as fragrant as the wood-chip varieties, its colors tend to clash, rather than complement, the flowers decorating the rim of the basket.

This *Victorian Lavender Basket* is both decorative and fragrant. The inside of the basket is lined with a Victorian-style floral print that is glue-gunned in place, and then filled with lavender potpourri.

To make the skirt, cut a length of fabric twice as long as the circumference of the basket. Form the gathers with elastic or running stitches, and hem the bottom. A glue gun quickly attaches the skirt to the basket, and rows of ribbon or lace can be attached with a glue gun or a sewing machine

This basket could easily be adapted for a wedding by using bird seed instead of potpourri, and choosing fabric to match the bride's dress.

This *Children's Potpourri Basket* is a decorative way to fragrance a bedroom.

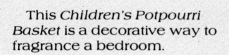

Begin by cutting a circle of fabric about four inches wider than the circumference of the basket. Turn the outer edges down to make a casing for ⅛" elastic. Now cut a piece of quilt batting the same size as the fabric. Place the fabric right-side down with the batting on top of it, and place the basket in the middle.

Lift the fabric and batting up together to cover the sides of the basket and stretch a piece of elastic through the casing until the fabric fits snugly around the basket's rim. The lace trim is attached with hot glue, and a bow made with matching lace is tied to the handle. The other side of the handle is decorated with a bouquet of silk peach rose-buds attached with hot glue.

The basket is filled with potpourri and topped with a doll dressed in matching lace.

(Tip: for a young child's room, place the potpourri basket on a dresser or shelf out of reach.)

This *Cinnamon Stick Basket* adds a spicy fragrance to any room. The basket is made from long cinnamon sticks, trimmed to the size you select, and can be filled with a small plant, herbs, or fresh strawberries.

Begin by cutting a square or rectangular base of heavy cardboard or thin plywood, and then start placing the cinnamon sticks with hot glue. Place one stick on each vertical side first, then one stick on each horizontal side. Repeat the process until you've built the basket up to a height you find pleasing.

The basket handle is made with a stem of artificial berries twisted around a length of heavy-gauge floral wire and hot-glued for reinforcement.

Concentrated cinnamon oil can be dabbed onto the cinnamon sticks to replenish the fragrance.

# *Holiday Baskets*

This *Summer Harvest Basket* celebrates the bounty of rich soil and makes a unique hostess gift for a cook-out or other summer activity.

Begin by tying a large bow made from paper ribbon around the center of the basket's handle. A trio of miniature scarecrows (available in craft supply or novelty shops) are then wired separately around their waists and attached to the center of the bow and on either side. Last, sprays of artificial raspberries are hot-glued around the handle.

The basket shown here is filled with red cabbage, corn, artichokes, and squash, but other garden produce would be equally attractive.

When you need some private time to wrap special gifts this holiday season, send the children out for a walk to find the natural materials needed to make this *Rustic Christmas Basket.*

Begin by white-washing a large oval basket and securing a large chunk of floral foam inside of it. Establish the lines of your arrangement by anchoring several large branches into the foam. Fill in the arrangement with sprays of pine and attach artificial red berries with hot glue.

Various shapes of pine cones and lichens are scattered throughout the basket, and a small bird's nest is placed among the pine cones. The red birds are attached to the branches last with hot glue.

A *Christmas Card Basket* is a festive way to display Christmas cards and adds holiday spirit to any room in the house.

Each side of the basket's handle is decorated with a branch of silk pine attached with floral wire. Sprays of artificial red berries are then arranged and wired into the greenery, and a bow is wired into the center of the arrangement.

Tip: to prevent unattractive wires from showing, cover them with a color of floral tape that will blend into the colors of your basket before wiring.

This *Pine Cone and Berries Basket* makes a beautiful holiday centerpiece. The basket can be left in a natural state, as shown here, or embellished further with glitter or tree ornaments. The basket can also be used as a fall or Thanksgiving centerpiece by filling it with gourds and colorful leaves.

Begin with a base of thick cardboard, thin plywood, or pine twigs wired together. You may luck out and find a perfectly curved branch for a handle, or you may have to cut a green branch, curve it to the shape you like, and allow it to dry.

The first row of pine cones is attached by forming a circle of heavy-gauge wire and wiring each pine cone individually to this circle with a thinner wire. When you've wired cones halfway around the basket, push one end of the handle flush with the base and wire it to the circle until you again come to the halfway point. Reinforce the handle ends and several of the pine cones to the base with hot glue.

The top row of cones are slightly smaller in size and use a smaller wire circle base, allowing them to tip inwards. Repeat the process described above and again hot-glue for reinforcement. Spray with a clear coat of shellac when finished. Plastic berry arrangements can be wired to the handle and scattered throughout the pine cones as a final touch.

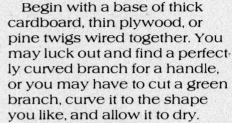

This *Christmas Gift Basket* is festive enough to substitute for a large tree if you live in a small apartment, or can be filled with gifts and delivered to someone in a rest home.

The basket can also be used to add holiday cheer to a hearth or used as a portable Christmas if you'll be traveling during the holidays.

Begin with a large, sturdy basket. Remove the stand from a small artificial tree and wire it to the basket in several places. Try to arrange the tree so the bottom branches are just above the basket's rim. The large velvet ribbon is attached next with hot glue.

The tree is then decorated with small ornaments and bows that coordinate with the packages.

This large *English Antique Basket* is decorated with a collection of old and new toys.

The toys are simply arranged in the basket until a pleasant design is achieved, and their edges then dabbed with hot glue to make the arrangement permanent.

The bow is then decorated with small Christmas novelties (attached with hot glue) and wired to the handle.

# Holiday Baskets

*Teddy's First Christmas Basket* makes a special gift for a favorite teacher or child.

Start by hot-gluing a strand of ribbon and lace around the outside of the basket. Then decorate the basket's handle by wrapping ribbon around it, using a spot of hot glue at the beginning and the end for reinforcement. Wire a small teddy bear (inexpensive at craft supply stores) to one side of the handle so that it appears to be sitting on the rim of the basket. The red ribbon around the bear's neck conceals the wire.

Underneath the bear, small sprigs of silk pine and dried German statice are hot-glued to the basket with miniature pine cones and red berries added as final accents. Last, a smaller arrangement of pine, statice, pine cones, and berries is glued to the opposite side of the basket.

This basket could also become a festive holiday centerpiece by filling it with Christmas peppermints or chocolates.

This *Holly and Cinnamon Christmas Basket* is small enough to add a touch of holiday cheer to any table or shelf in the house, and can be filled with candy canes or chocolates.

Begin by tightly twisting a handful of Spanish moss and hot-gluing it to the rim of your basket. Then wrap a length of festive ribbon around the handle, hot-gluing it at the beginning and the end for reinforcement.

Now glue four clusters of cinnamon sticks to your moss base, trying to space them as evenly as possible. Glue four small bows onto each group of cinnamon.

To attach the silk holly, dab a small amount of hot glue on the bottom of a stem and insert it into the moss at an angle. Repeat the process all the way around the basket's rim, taking care to always insert the holly at the same angle. Fill in any bare spots with dried German statice and garnish with red silk berries.

This *Easter Centerpiece Basket* is large enough to look nice on a long coffee table or in an entrance way.

Instead of plastic Easter grass, the basket is filled with Spanish moss that has been spray painted with teal paint for a more natural look. A small piece of floral foam is hidden underneath the moss on one side, and silk flowers and greenery are inserted into it. (Tip: if you'd prefer fresh flowers in your basket, check floral supply stores for water-soaked oasis or water tubes that can be hidden under the moss.) A yellow bow is wired to the handle, and antique Easter eggs and note cards are arranged in the basket.

This *Easter Gift Basket* makes a special gift for someone in a hospital or rest home during the Easter season.

The basket is first spray painted pink and then white washed. To make the arrangement, secure a large chunk of floral foam inside the basket with wire or hot glue. Form a bouquet by inserting stems of silk, paper, or dried flowers into the foam and covering any bare spots with moss. The stuffed bunny is attached to the handle with wire, and silk cord is used to make several looping bows.

This *Iridescent Easter Basket* brings a very contemporary form of holiday cheer.

The basket is first painted with metal flake auto paint, and then filled with a block of floral foam hot-glued in place. The foam is covered with shredded strips of mylar or white Easter grass.

Next, a handful of plastic eggs are colored first with craft spray paint and then with a layer of iridescent sparkle spray paint. The eggs are secured in the basket with hot glue, and artificial leaves and berry branches (also sprayed with metallic paint) are arranged in the basket.

This *Silk Dogwood Easter Basket* brightens the home with a celebration of spring.

A length of floral wire is first wrapped with green floral tape for a more natural appearance and then used to attach two stems of silk dogwood and one stem of silk ivy to the basket. The filling is shredded pink raffia, available in craft supply stores.

This *Harvest Horn Basket* makes a traditional Thanksgiving cornucopia to decorate a coffee table or counter top.

Begin by cutting a chunk of floral foam to fit inside the basket. The bow is then wired and inserted into the top of the foam, and the flower stems are inserted to form the arrangement.

The dried and silk flowers include: eucalyptus, bittersweet, baby's breath, sweet Annie, yarrow, and hill flowers.

This *Heart and Arrow Valentine Basket* is quick to make and uses a commercially prepared pink and grey heart-shaped basket.

The dried wheat stalks (purchased pre-dyed) are arranged in an arrow shape, with a few of the shafts wired together in the back to help maintain the shape. The wheat bouquet is then wired to the basket at the bottom, and the bow is wired next to it. Once you have the materials in hand, this charming basket takes less than five minutes to make.

This pair of *Floral Heart Baskets* illustrates the variety of basket shapes and sizes available in five and dime and craft stores.

The baskets are decorated by hot-gluing strips of tightly twisted Spanish moss around the rim to form a base, and then adding dried flowers by dabbing a bit of hot glue on each stem and inserting it into the moss at an angle.

The dried flowers include: baby's breath, celosia, roses, globe amaranth, larkspur, pearly everlasting, nigella, statice, and dyed pepper grass.

# Holiday Baskets

This *New Year's Eve Cele-bration Basket* makes a festive hostess gift for a party, or a great invitation for a more private celebration.

Begin by spray painting a light layer of silver paint onto a large basket. Artificial pine boughs or other greenery you plan to use can be sprayed at the same time.

Cut a large chunk of floral foam and secure it inside the basket with wire and/or hot glue. Push a champagne hold-er (available in wine stores) down into the floral foam and insert the champagne bottle.

Now arrange your frosted greenery around the cham-pagne and anchor it in the floral foam. Hot-glue several silver tree ornaments into the arrangement and top with a large white and silver bow.

# Culinary & Dining

This *Victorian Picnic Basket* reflects the Victorian tradition of doing even the simplest things —such as a picnic — in elaborate style.

The picnic basket is decorated by tying bows of white lace onto each side of the handle. One bow is then embellished with delicate ferns, while the other bow is built into a rose bouquet made from ferns, silk leaves, a small piece of tulle, a small bow, and a pearl corsage pin.

Additional lengths of lace are then cut to make bows to tie around the wine glasses and the napkins.

This basket would make an unusual wedding gift, and the plates and glasses could be chosen to match the bride's registered setting.

The decorative handle of this *Summer Fruit Basket* provides an unconventional twist to the traditional fruit basket. The base of the basket is packed with excelsior, and the fruit is placed on top of it. (Tip: green Easter grass also looks nice.) Decorate the handle by hot-gluing sprays of artificial plums, apples, and peaches onto the basket, filling in any bare areas with dried German statice.

This *Brass Centerpiece Basket* is a beautiful reminder of the endless variety of materials used to make baskets.

The basket is filled with freeze-dried lettuce, asparagus, and strawberries. A large French ribbon (regular ribbon lined with thin wire to help maintain shaping) is then tied into a bow on one side of the basket, with freeze-dried strawberries hot-glued into the bow as accents.

The chocolate fondue basket, left, is decorated on the outside with marshmallows, strawberries, and large chocolate chips attached with hot glue. (Tip: since marshmallows and chocolate tend to melt when the hot glue is applied, do not make this basket too far in advance, and be sure to handle it gently.) The marshmallows are then decorated with shaved chocolate, and any bare spots are filled in with vanilla cookies attached with toothpicks. The inside of the basket is filled with bananas, apples, marshmallows, grapes, strawberries, and vanilla cookies. Two smaller baskets, lined with cupcake tins, are filled with melted chocolate for dipping.

Surprise your next guests with a deviation from the usual hors d'oeuvres with this festive pair of *Fondue Baskets*.

The outside of the **cheese** fondue basket, right, is decorated with vegetables skewered on toothpicks and then tucked into open areas in the handle. The basket is filled with red peppers, celery, mushrooms, and carrots. Two smaller baskets are lined with cupcake tins and filled with cheese fondue for dipping.

This beautiful *Chocolate Lover's Basket*, filled with fruit-shaped truffles, makes a beautiful party centerpiece and can be eaten as a dessert!

To make the basket you'll need: several squares of tempered chocolate (available in stores selling candy-making supplies), one balloon, and a pastry bag with a small tip.

Begin by blowing the balloon up to the size you'd like your finished basket to be. Melt the chocolate and pour into a bowl that's wide enough to accommodate the balloon with ease. Dip the balloon about halfway into the chocolate and gently

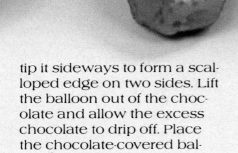

tip it sideways to form a scalloped edge on two sides. Lift the balloon out of the chocolate and allow the excess chocolate to drip off. Place the chocolate-covered balloon on a serving platter and allow to cool. (Note: some of the chocolate will drip down and form a base at the bottom of the basket.)

Create the handle by filling a pastry bag about half full with melted chocolate and outlining the shape of your handle with chocolate. Fill in with the decorative pattern of your choice. Decorate the sides of the basket by first adding a row of chocolate around the outer edges of the basket and then adding decorative patterns underneath it. After the handle and sides have dried, trace over your outline and patterns with a second layer of chocolate. When the second layer of chocolate has dried, slowly deflate the balloon and discard.

This *Ultimate Picnic Basket* can be delivered to a special friend as a luncheon invitation or given as a bride's basket for an engagement gift.

First, search out a basket with an unusual shape and then simply tie a pair of wine glasses and an antique linen napkin into a length of ribbon tied around the basket's handle. The ribbon is hot-glued in strategic locations for reinforcement.

Although this *Sandwich Basket* is very delicate and will not last forever, it does make an attractive serving platter for a luncheon party.

The basket is made by hot-gluing pretzel and sesame sticks together into a log cabin pattern, and gluing them to a base

of heavy cardboard or thin plywood. The handle is then made from large bread sticks, also glued in place.

A linen napkin can be folded to disguise the base, and finger sandwiches are arranged around the basket.

The Christmas colors and fragrant evergreen potpourri used to decorate this *Culinary Gift Basket* makes it a basket worth keeping after the gifts have been removed.

Begin with a ten-cent vegetable basket and spray paint it the color of your choice. Cut two rectangular pieces of fabric large enough to line the inside of the basket and drape over the sides. Place the first layer of fabric right-side down and glue the corners. Sprinkle an even layer of potpourri over it and cover with a second piece of fabric, this time placed right-side up. Spot glue the corners and edges; then play with the fabric, draping it over the sides until you have a shape you like, and hot-glue in place with the raw edges folded under.

This unusual *Vegetable Bouquet Basket* uses freeze-dried vegetables and other natural materials to make a decorative basket for a kitchen countertop.

The twig basket is first decorated with stripped honey-suckle vines that are tied in place with raffia. Vegetable bouquets are then formed with spring onions, mushrooms, red cabbage, and Spanish moss, and secured together with hot glue.

This *Apples and Daisies Fruit Basket* makes a decorative table or kitchen counter centerpiece.

The leaves from a large artificial plant are first trimmed off and then hot-glued at different angles around the basket. The handle is decorated by rolling the leaves around it tightly and hot-gluing them in place.

The branch of daisies is attached with wire that has been covered first with green floral tape.

Since the leaves completely cover the basket's surface, this is an ideal project for a damaged or unattractive basket.

The unusual shape of this *Freeze-Dried Fruit Basket* is enhanced by the designer's creative use of paper ribbon.

The ribbon, which comes in tightly rolled strips, is woven around the weft (horizontal) strips of the basket, and then opened up at the corners and tied into a ribbon.

Freeze-dried peaches and strawberries are then hot-glued to the bow. The basket can be filled with gifts or filled with table napkins and used as a table centerpiece.

The oval shapes of many fruits naturally lend themselves to becoming *Party Fruit Baskets.*

Begin with a clean, dry watermelon. Place it on a flat surface and allow it to roll until it stops. Use a crayon or marker to outline the shape of your basket and follow your marks with a sharp paring knife. You can also design the zigzag edge in this way. The cantaloupe and honeydew melon baskets are easier to make without handles.

Use the top half of these melons and the cutaway sections of the watermelon to make the melon balls. (Look for melon-ballers in grocery and department stores.) For a large party, you may want to purchase additional melons so you'll have extra melon balls to refill the fruit basket.

The grapefruit basket is made in the same way as the watermelon basket (minus the zigzag edges) and filled with strawberries. (Tip: do not pick fruit baskets up by their handles.)

This *Condiment Basket* makes a beautiful table arrangement and also saves space. Customize the basket to your own home by coordinating the napkin, greenery, and floral colors to those in your dining area.

Begin the basket by hot-gluing a small block of floral foam inside one end of the basket and covering it with Spanish moss using floral pins. Next, insert your silk flowers and greenery into the foam (a silk lantana bush is shown here), and fill the basket with condiments and napkins.

These *Miniature Floral Bouquet Baskets* make lovely place settings for a dinner party and can be given to each guest as a keepsake of the evening.

To duplicate the baskets shown here, cut several chunks of floral foam, insert them into the baskets, and cover the foam with Spanish moss. Insert the stems of dried statice, pink yarrow, thyme, sea lavender, and baby's breath into the floral foam. Delicate flowers, such as the globe amaranth and roses, will need to have their stems wired with a thin-gauged floral wire for strength before inserting into the floral foam.

Fill in any bare spots with dried greenery, and spray on a light coating of regular hairspray to prevent shattering.

These *Candlelight Centerpiece Baskets* are easy to make and can be color coordinated to any home's decor. Place the baskets side by side on a smaller dining table or spread them out over the length of a larger table.

The smaller, outer baskets are each filled with a small piece of floral foam that is hot-glued to the basket's inside bottom. Small plastic candle holders are pushed into each basket's foam, and the foam is then covered with pinned moss. Silk greenery and crocus are inserted into the foam on the outside edges, and decorative stones are added for weight.

The larger, center basket is made in the same way, with the greenery and crocus arranged evenly around the basket. Finally, the candles are inserted into the candle holders.

Tip: before lighting the candles, make sure the greenery and the basket will not come in contact with the flame as the candles burn down.

# Bedroom & Bath

This *Finger Towel Basket* uses three basket decorating techniques to create the ultimate in bathroom decor.

The basket is first painted white with spray enamel. The chintz lining can be customized to match any color scheme, and the gathers are formed and held in place by running a heavy wire through a fabric casing just below the rim line.

To attach the dried flowers, a base of tightly twisted Spanish moss is first glued to the rim of the basket. The flower stems are then dabbed with hot glue and individually inserted into the moss. The flowers include: German statice, larkspur, roses, pearly everlasting, celosia, straw-flowers, hydrangea, and globe amaranth.

As a final touch, chintz bows were added to the sides of the handle, with small bouquets of dried flowers hot-glued in place.

This *Victorian Bathroom Basket* is a beautiful way to fragrance your bathroom.

The basket is decorated by cutting a circle of fabric about four inches wider than the circumference of the basket. Turn the outer edges down to make a casing for ⅛" elastic. Now cut a piece of quilt batting the same size as the fabric. Place the fabric right-side down with the batting on top of it, and place the basket in the middle.

Lift the fabric and batting up together to cover the sides of the basket, and stretch a piece of elastic through the casing until the fabric fits snugly around the basket's rim. A row of gathered lace is added next with hot glue, and small satin roses are glued to the rim.

Scented soaps in a variety of shapes are then covered in floral fabric and tied with satin ribbon.

This lacy *Lingerie Basket* forms a decorative storage area. Made in different fabrics and colors the basket can also be used in the kitchen to store napkins and silverware or in the bathroom to store guest towels and soaps.

Begin by painting a lidded basket the color of your choice. Cut a piece of fabric to fit the top and bottom of the basket, and then use the fabric as a pattern to cut matching pieces of quilt batting. Hot-glue the batting and lining to the insides, and trim with lace. Pockets are made by trimming a strip of horizontal fabric with lace and hot-gluing the edges to the top of the basket.

Baskets similar to this *Victorian Trinket Basket* were used to hold house keys and jewelry in Victorian days.

Start with a piece of fabric cut to fit the inside of your basket. Use this fabric as a pattern to cut a piece of quilt batting, and hot-glue the batting to the inside of the basket. Hot-glue the fabric over the batting, right-side up, and allow the raw edges to overlap the basket's rim.

Now form a fabric skirt by cutting a length of fabric twice the circumference of the basket. Form gathers with elastic or running stitches, and hot-glue around the rim, covering the raw edges of the lining. Add a row of gathered lace and hot-glue in place.

The basket is trimmed with bows of silk ribbon, and silk flowers are attached with hot glue. The matching sachet heart can be filled with potpourri or quilt batting.

The unusual shape of this *Bathroom Wall Basket* makes it ideal for holding decorative soaps.

Before choosing the items you'll be decorating with, make a careful study of your current bathroom decor. Is there a color or theme in your wallpaper that you'd like to pick up?

The basket shown here begins by wiring a floral print bow to the top of the basket and lining the inside of the basket with coordinating tissue paper. Seashells that match the designer's wallpaper are then hot-glued around the bow and the top rim of the basket.

This *Children's Bathroom Wall Basket* is decorated with a few favorite toys and makes a creative toothbrush holder.

The outside of the basket is stomping ground for dinosaurs (attached with hot glue) and small green frogs (attached with wire). The inside of the basket is a safe retreat for a pair of teddy bear soaps.

A length of ribbon is then threaded through the side of the basket and tied in a bow. A loop in the bow is used to hang the basket on the wall.

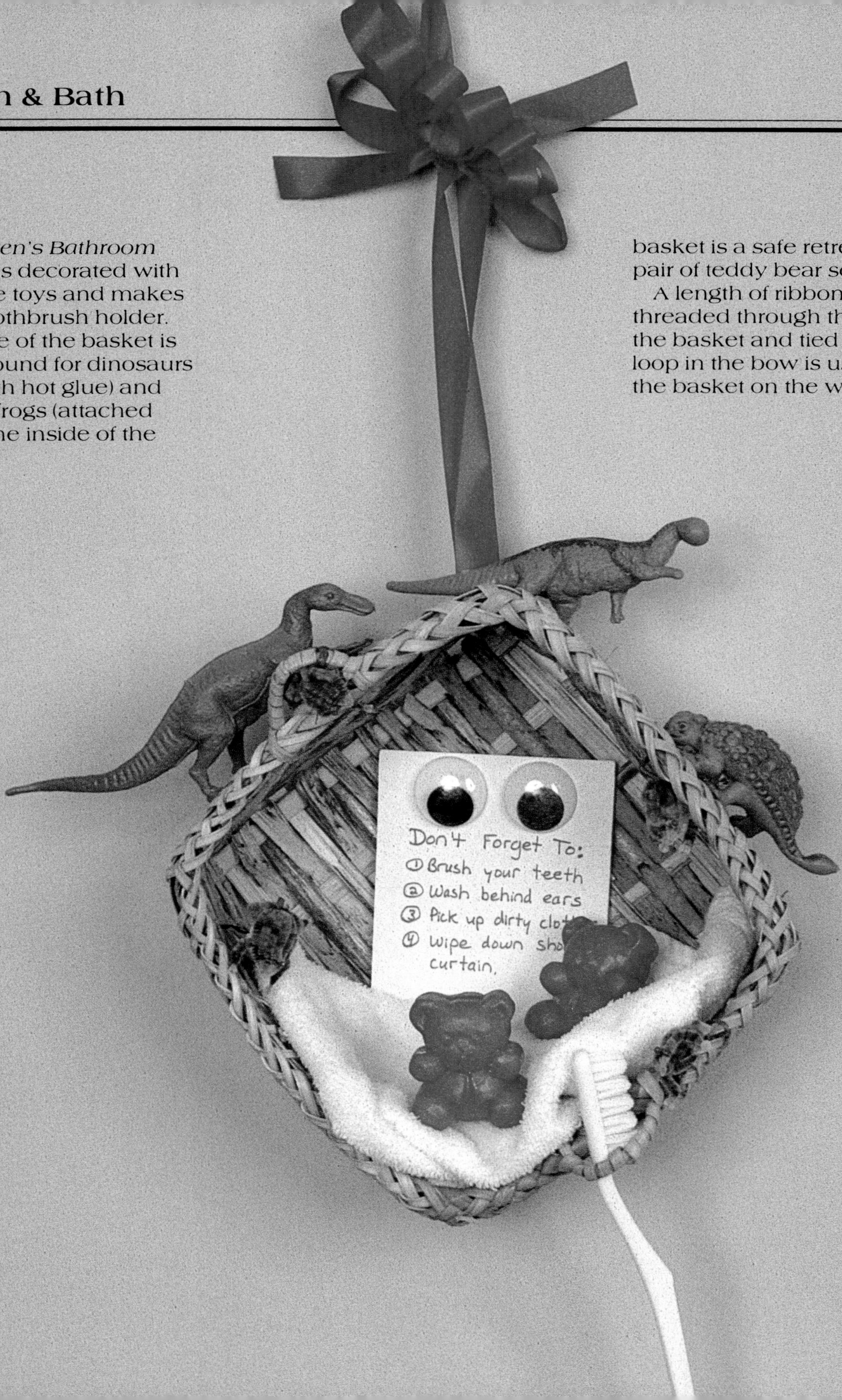

Don't Forget To:
① Brush your teeth
② Wash behind ears
③ Pick up dirty cloth
④ Wipe down sho
    curtain.

This *Miniature Moss and Roses Basket* is more challenging to make than the larger moss basket shown on page 32 because of the tight corners. The sheet moss is not as delicate as you might imagine, though, so don't be afraid to experiment.

The moss is glue-gunned to the inside of the basket first. The basket's outside surface is worked next, with care taken to molding the moss to the basket's form and preventing any seams from showing. (Tip: to make your seams match, tear your sheet moss instead of cutting it with scissors. The jagged edges blend together more naturally.) The basket is then trimmed with roses and the ribbon is attached with a glue gun.

Moss-covered baskets are beautiful when filled with potpourri or plants. Try to remember, though, that the moss is still living and will turn brown if exposed to direct sunlight.

This *Floral Tabletop Basket* is made with an ordinary wicker bread basket and bread dough flowers.

The basket is first painted in peach paint and then white-washed. The bread dough flower pieces (available in craft supply stores) are first painted with craft paints and then hot-glued to the basket in a pleasant arrangement.

This *Victorian Boudoir Basket* is made from an ordinary wicker bread basket.

Start with a circular piece of fabric cut to fit the bottom of the basket with a large flower or other print in the center of it. Use the fabric circle as a pattern to cut a piece of quilt batting. Hot-glue the batting to the bottom of the basket and then hot-glue the fabric on top of the batting.

The inside edges of the basket are then decorated with a length of two- to three-inch gathered lace hot-glued in place. The basket is trimmed by weaving satin stream-ers around the rim and hot-gluing a small bouquet of silk roses at the center.

This *Decorated Cosmetic Basket* is an attractive way to organize favorite cosmetics and perfumes.

Begin by spray painting a rectangular basket pink and applying a white wash. Weave a strand of beads loosely

around the basket, using hot glue in strategic places for reinforcement. A bouquet of paper or silk flowers is then arranged and hot-glued to one corner of each side of the basket.

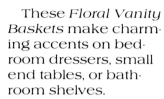

These *Floral Vanity Baskets* make charming accents on bedroom dressers, small end tables, or bathroom shelves.

The top basket was first decorated with a splattered finish. The dried flowers (chosen because their colors match so well) are then attached by hot-gluing a base of tightly twisted Spanish moss around the rim of the basket and gluing them into the moss. The dried flowers include: German statice, purple statice, globe amaranth, and raspberry thistle.

The basket below was first prepared with a glaze over a peach base coat. The ribbon is then wrapped around the basket (secured in the back with a dab of hot glue) and tied in a bow. Last, small sprigs of dried hydrangea are hot-glued into the ribbon.

These small *Bathroom Trinket Baskets* can be filled with practical items, such as cotton balls, or used for decorative appeal.

The square basket on the left is decorated with pieces of dried protea, sumac, rose hips, and sweet Annie that are arranged in a mosaic pattern and attached with hot glue.

The cotton ball basket, right, is decorated with rows of ribbon attached with hot glue, and a bow with sprigs of dried German statice arranged and glued to the top.

Place this *Wishing Well Basket* in your bedroom and use it to collect leftover pocket change.

Purchased for under five dollars in a craft supply store, the basket is both inexpensive and quick to decorate. The dollar bill is first accordion-folded and stapled to the basket. (Floral wire could be used instead of the staples.) Small coins are placed around the rim with hot glue, and as a final touch, a small wish basket is threaded through a ribbon and hung over the dollar bill to cover the staple.

This *Keepsake Valentine Basket* is decorated by decoupaging a picture cut out from a cherished Valentine card.

Begin by coating the outside of the basket with decoupage medium (available in craft supply stores). Use hot glue to attach the picture of your choice to the basket, and then coat with another layer of decoupage medium.

The arrangement is made by cutting a chunk of floral foam to fit the inside of the basket and inserting a bouquet of dried baby's breath in it.

# *Around the Home*

The two baskets shown here reveal a clever way to decorate antique baskets without damaging their delicate fibers. The bows are first assembled on a work table, with decorative items attached into the bow with hot glue. After the glue has dried, the bows are attached to the baskets with wire.

The large *Fireplace Wood Basket*, right, is decorated with a bow of stripped honeysuckle vine with sponge mushrooms and galex arranged and hot-glued to it.

The small *Country Hearth Basket*, left, is decorated with a bow of ribbon with freeze-dried vegetables (string beans and radishes) hot-glued into it.

Decorative as a floral arrangement or coffee table centerpiece, this *Magazine Basket* also prevents your favorite reading materials from becoming an eyesore.

Begin by wrapping several lengths of medium-gauge floral wire with green floral tape. Then use the wrapped wire to attach several sprigs of silk greenery to the basket. With a little creative maneuvering of the foliage, you can even keep the wire from showing.

This *Pastel Floral Basket* uses a heart-shaped basket to create a very romantic look.

Begin by loosely wrapping a length of peach ribbon around the handle and hot-gluing at each end for reinforcement. Repeat with an aqua ribbon. The aqua bow is attached to the center of the heart with wire.

Now form a base around the rim with tightly twisted Spanish moss secured with hot glue. Cluster together several stems of baby's breath, dab them with hot glue, and insert them into the moss at an angle.

Spray several clusters of baby's breath with aqua spray paint and insert them randomly around the base. Next make several small bows with peach ribbon and hot-glue them to the baby's breath. Last, hot-glue the aqua bird to the handle and glue a streamer of peach ribbon to his beak.

This *Plant Stand Basket* is decorated with craft markers and uses the vertical slats as miniature picture frames.

The designs were traced from magazines and then transferred to the basket with carbon paper. Acrylic or oil paints can be used instead of markers if your design is not extremely detailed.

The *Oak Americana Basket* shown here was designed by its patriotic owner to be displayed beneath an American wall flag.

The large bow is attached first with wire, and its streamers are then draped down each side of the basket's rim and hot-glued in selected areas for reinforcement. Dried eucalyptus, German statice, and tiltree are hot-glued around the bow. (Tip: tuck some of the dried materials under the bow for a more natural appearance.) The birds are then hot-glued among the flowers, and a small branch of dried tiltree is glued to each bird's beak for an extra touch.

A small piece of floral foam hot-glued to the side of the basket and covered with moss keeps the basket sitting at an attractive angle.

The beautiful surface design of this *Match Collection Basket* mirrors the colors of a match flame.

The basket begins with an unfinished wood slat basket. The base coat is applied with peach craft spray paint, and then gradated tones of yellow, peach, orange, red, dark blue, and light blue are applied in rows with craft spray paint. (Tip: craft spray paints come in a wider variety of color tones than ordinary spray paints.)

After the gradated tones have dried, a layer of iridescent sparkle spray is applied, and the basket is lined with shredded mylar.

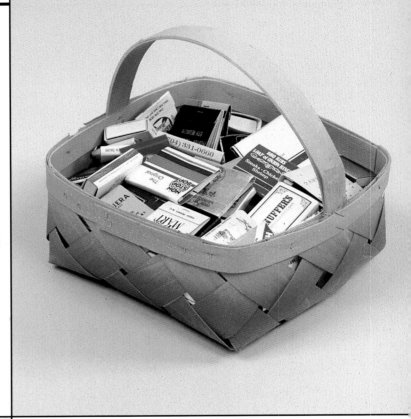

An inexpensive wicker basket can easily be transformed into this *Ivy and Ribbon Trash Basket* in less than an hour.

Create the verdigris finish by applying a coat of dark green acrylic paint diluted with water with a sponge. After it has dried, sponge on a second coat of light green paint diluted with water.

Form a bow with cotton ribbon or with fabric dipped in fabric stiffener. Attach the bow to the basket with wire and use hot glue to secure the bow's streamers in place. Arrange silk or paper ivy vines around the ribbon with hot glue or wire.

This *Floral Bow Basket* uses half a yard of a floral print fabric and some fabric stiffener to form a cheerful basket that would look nice any-where in the home.

Start with a white basket with a tall handle. Fold a strip of fabric to a width you think will complement the size of your basket's handle, and dip it in a commercially prepared fabric stiffener (available in craft supply stores). Drape your stiffened fabric over the handle and form a bow. Apply weights or hold in place by hand until the fabric has dried.

As an extra touch, this basket's designer cut out flowers from scraps of her fabric, dipped them in the stiffener, and then applied them to the basket. After drying, a clear coat of sealer or varnish was applied to the outside of the basket.

This *Guest Bedroom Basket* is decorated on both the outside and the inside with dried flower arrangements.

The bouquet inside the basket begins with a small block of floral foam wired to one end of the basket. The dried flowers — poppy pods, pink and white larkspur, lavender, and ti tree blossoms — are inserted by their stems into the floral foam. The other end of the basket can be filled with guest towels, reading materials, etc.

The bouquet outside the basket is made by hot-gluing small pieces of the dried flowers to the outside of the basket, beginning in the center and working up towards the rim.

This *Camper's Memory Basket* uses items found around the campsite or in the woods to decorate a basket.

The inside of the basket is decorated by stair-stepping mushrooms up one side, and filling in bare areas with moss and fungus. The items are attached with hot glue. The outside of the basket is decorated with various mushrooms, fungi, seed pods, and mosses, also attached with hot glue. (Tip: if you have small children in your home, be sure to avoid poisonous mushrooms. Dried mushrooms can also be purchased in many craft supply stores.)

This *Antique Lover's Basket* is simple
to decorate and looks lovely on a small
corner table.

The basket is first sprayed with a light
layer of silver spray paint. A base is then
formed by hot-gluing a length of tightly
twisted Spanish moss around the rim.
Small stems of dried caspia are then
dabbed with hot glue and inserted
at an angle into the moss one at a
time. Stems of dried eucalyptus
are added in the same way.
(Tip: the dried eucalyptus
can be spray painted to
any color you like.)

# Around the Home

Simple to make, mail baskets are both functional and decorative. The *Garden Mail Basket*, above left, is made by attaching a small cube of floral foam inside a basket with hot glue. The foam cube is then covered with moss (secured with floral pins) for a more natural appearance, and a sprig of silk ivy is inserted. The paper ribbon is wired to the basket and a small wire hook attached for hanging.

The *Personalized Address Basket*, below left, sparkles with patriotism and practicality. The basket's inside is decorated with a red quilted fabric that is fitted to the basket's form and then hot-glued in place. The red, white, and blue ribbon is woven into the basket's warp and the bow reinforced with hot glue. A rectangle of coordinating needlepoint attaches simply with hot glue, and can be easily pulled off and replaced with a new address if the owner moves.

This *Teddy Bear Playground Basket* can be used to deliver birthday presents, store small toy pieces, or decorate a child's room.

The playground is formed with Spanish moss that is tightly twisted and hot-glued to the rim. Small alphabet blocks, plastic shape blocks, toy cars, and nuts are then hot-glued around the basket.

The miniature teddy bears (available in craft supply and novelty shops) are then positioned around the toys and attached with hot glue.

This *Children's Coloring Basket* makes a decorative organizer for crayons and other art supplies.

The crayons are hot-glued in place one at a time, with small clusters of crayons arranged and hot-glued around the handle.

Since the crayons cover the majority of the basket's outer surface, this is an ideal project for a damaged or unattractive basket.

This *Parent's Revenge Basket* puts creative use to years of accumulated knickknacks from gumball machines and carnival games.

To create visual variety, hot-glue some of the items in random order, while arranging others to form scenes and then hot-gluing. Some of the scenes on the basket shown here include: airplane and car crashes, black ants chasing flamingos, fish swimming upside down with worms on them, a scorpion crawling over a graveyard of skeletons, peanuts with wild sheep walking on them, toy soldiers confronting dogs guarding their doghouses, and bells wearing sunglasses.

This *Floral Trinket Basket* is a decorative way to hide the everyday clutter of coupons, unread mail, and other small items.

Begin with an inexpensive wood fruit basket and spray paint it the color of your choice. Sinuata, strawflowers, and poppies are then arranged to appear growing on a stem and hot-glued to the basket.

This *Floral Wreath Basket* is small enough to decorate a kitchen shelf or bathroom counter, and can be made in colors to coordinate with any room.

Begin by hot-gluing a base of tightly twisted Spanish moss to the rim of the basket. Trim a branch of dried German statice into two- or three-inch strips and glue them into the moss at an angle all the way around the basket. Stems of dried clover are attached next, and the more delicate dried flowers (baby's breath and pepper grass) are attached last.

These small *Ribbon Baskets* can be decorated in less than five minutes once you have all the materials on hand.

The gathered ribbon can be purchased by the yard in fabric and craft stores with the lace already attached. The ribbon is simply hot-glued around the rim of the basket and a coordinating ribbon attached with wire.

For an interesting variation of the common floral wreath basket, this *Delphinium Centerpiece Basket* is decorated on the basket's side instead of the rim.

Begin by wiring a piece of floral foam to one side of a basket and covering it with Spanish moss using greening pins. Then simply insert your flower stems into the foam to create an arrangement. (Tip: delicate stems may need to be wrapped with a thin-gauged floral wire before inserting into the foam.)

The dried flowers include: delphinium, maple pods, pearly everlasting, and several varieties of grasses.

# *Hanging Baskets*

This trio of *Nantucket Wall Baskets* illustrates the wide variety of basket styles available. The baskets were made from willow and reed and were stained to achieve their dark color.

**Right:** Sphagnum moss is first layered over the flat reeds and glued down lightly with a water-based glue. The flower stems are then inserted into the moss while the glue is still wet. (Tip: stems can be wired with a thin-gauged floral wire if they need to be stronger.)

The dried flowers include: sea lavender, caspia, springeri fern, German statice, German myrtle, poppy seed heads, blue salvia, daisies, Dutch iris, wild yarrow, artemesia, and sweet Annie.

**Left:** The small pocket in this basket is first filled with pieces of floral foam. The foam is then covered on all sides with sphagnum moss (other types of moss work just as well) to prevent the foam from showing through the basket's weave.

The dried flowers are then inserted into the foam. They include: caspia, German statice, sea statice, boxwood, daffodils, Dutch iris, daisies, Spartan roses, fern, poppy heads, lavender, blue salvia, and silver king artemesia.

The bow is attached last with wire.

**Right:** The basket is first prepared with sphagnum moss in the same way as the first basket. For variety, a small piece of moss is glued to the outside of the basket beside the arrangement.

The dried flowers include: German statice, caspia, lavender, poppy seeds, Spartan roses, daisies, iris greenery, and sea statice.

This scenic *Goose-on-the-Loose Basket* uses a shadow box effect to make an unusual wall hanging.

The nature scene is created by hot-gluing a tree fungus in one corner of the basket and inserting eucalyptus, bead corn, and dried caspia into it. A handful of moss is glued next to the tree fungus, and then the goose is placed and hot-glued.

The loose weave of this *Country Wheel Basket* allows you to decorate the middle of the basket while still leaving enough space for the background (such as a wallpaper print) to show through.

A large bow is first wired to the center of the basket. Small pieces of dried German statice are then hot-glued into the outer edges of the bow to form a base, and sprigs of pepper grass and silk peach flowers are hot-glued into the statice.

This basket is flat enough to fit in the narrow space between a storm door and an outer door without damaging the arrangement.

This pair of *Lovebird Baskets* is a fun wedding or anniversary gift to make for special friends.

Available in craft supply and novelty stores, the birds are easily attached to the baskets with a spot of hot glue, and can be positioned to appear gazing at each other.

Sprigs of dried German statice, globe amaranth, and baby's breath are hot-glued around the birds. As a special touch, a small piece of globe amaranth can be hot-glued onto one of the bird's beak.

This *Spring Door Basket* is a festive welcome sign to visitors and is flat enough to fit between a storm door and an outer door.

Begin by tightly twisting a handful of Spanish moss and hot-gluing it along the rim. The bow is then wired into the corner, and small silk flowers and greenery are glued around the bow's edges and across the rim. Once you have the ingredients in hand, this basket takes less than ten minutes to make.

This scenic *Nesting Birds Basket* starts with a simple, inexpensive basket with the handle removed.

To achieve a natural look, the birds (available in craft supply and novelty stores) are glued onto the basket first. The bows are added next, with the ribbons trailing from the baby birds down to the mother bird. A small bouquet of dried baby's breath and pepper grass is then glued in between the baby birds, and a larger bouquet of these same flowers is glued around the mother bird and the bow.

The designer of this *Broom Corn Basket* was enchanted by the commercially prepared surface of the basket and decided to use the basket as a prop for a forest scene.

A simple raffia bow is first wired to the side of the basket, and small branches of birch are hot-glued into the bow. The birds are added last with hot glue, and from start to finish the basket takes less than five minutes to decorate!

# Basket Arrangements

pick your own moss, be sure to cook it in a microwave oven for about 45 seconds after it has dried to kill any small insects. Place a small container of water next to the moss while it's cooking to prevent over-drying.)

The dried flower stems are reinforced with a thin-gauged wire and then covered with floral tape. (Tip: inserting the stems into the foam is simpler if you leave the last inch or two of the stem un-taped.)

The dried flowers include: Ambassador roses, wild daisies, pink strawflowers, hydrangea, dianthus, camomile, asparagus fern, caspia, lavender, blue salvia, and English ivy.

The bouquet is preserved by spraying a light layer of inexpensive hairspray over flowers about once a month. Avoid displaying the arrangement in direct sunlight to prevent the colors from fading.

This *Wicker Basket Arrangement* is a "tour de force" in dried flowers. The arrangement is made slightly off-center so it can be viewed from more than one angle.

Begin by wrapping a length of taffeta ribbon diagonally around the basket's handle. Secure the ribbon with a dab of hot glue at the beginning and the end.

Now cut a piece of floral foam to fit the bottom of the basket and cover it with moss. (Tip: if you decide to

This *Victorian Nosegay Basket* creates an old-fashioned look with dried and paper flowers.

A chunk of floral foam is first cut to the size of the basket and secured with hot glue or wire. The largest and tallest flowers are inserted first, and the smaller flowers used to fill out the arrangement. The dried flowers include: lavender, baby rosebuds, German statice, and globe amaranth.

The natural colors in this *Pheasant Feather and Pod Basket Arrangement* are unobtrusive and would blend in with almost any decor.

A piece of floral foam is first cut to the size of the basket and secured with hot glue. Tall pheasant feathers are used to establish the height parameters of the arrangement, while smaller feathers are used to create width. Last, miniature lotus pods are inserted into the arrangement to provide visual variety and fill in the bare spots.

Baskets like this *Antique Bark Basket* were used for many years by American Indians for herb-gathering excursions.

The pine cones in this basket are hot-glued on their edges to help keep the arrangement in place, while the outside of the basket is decorated with a vine of silk leaves and berries and a small tree bracket. (Tip: to avoid hot-gluing the vine and bracket to the outside of the basket and risking damage to the antique, wrap a length of heavy-gauge floral wire around the vine to help keep its shape, and attach the bracket to the wire with hot glue.)

This *Paper Flower Arrangement Basket* illustrates the amazing beauty of paper flowers.

The basket is decorated by dipping a square of fabric in fabric stiffener (available in craft sup-

The basket for this *Paper Roses and Dogwood Arrangement Basket* was a real flea market find.

A chunk of floral foam is first cut to fit the basket and secured with hot glue. The paper flowers and greenery are then inserted into the front part of the floral foam. Tall branches of dried flowers are inserted into the back of the foam for height and fullness.

After you've finished your arrangement, the paper flowers can be shaped to appear in bud form, all the way open, or anything in between.

ply stores), molding it around the bottom of the basket, and tying with silk cord.

The arrangement is made by cutting a chunk of floral foam to fit the inside of the basket and securing it with hot glue. The paper flowers and greenery are inserted into the foam and arranged in the same way silk or dried flowers would be.

This *Blooming Peaches Arrangement Basket* is a beautiful centerpiece for a summer barbecue or family reunion.

Create the gradated tones on the basket's surface by spray painting a base coat of peach craft paint and then applying spray painted rows of light yellow, dark yellow, orange, peach, coral, and crimson craft paint from the top down. When the gradated tones have dried, splatter a small amount of crimson paint over the row of yellow, and then splatter a small amount of yellow over the crimson.

Create the arrangement by cutting a block of floral foam to fit the basket and hot-gluing it in place. Last, hot-glue artificial peaches around the basket, inserting small sprays of paper peach blossoms into the foam around the peaches.

A *Spring Fling Basket* makes a novel centerpiece that can be custom designed to flatter any home. The basket rests on its side and is decorated with two separate arrangements. (Tip: a long-handled basket works best for this type of arrangement.)

The back of the basket is decorated by wiring several artificial flower bulbs (see inset) into the basket and hot-gluing them for reinforcement. A sponge mushroom is hot-glued underneath the bulbs, and touches of Spanish moss are tucked in to hide the bare spots. Silk daffodils are inserted into the bulbs.

The arrangement inside the basket begins with a peach bow glued onto a block of floral foam that is then glued into the basket. Dried pussy willows, pepper grass, and caspia are inserted into the foam in a fan shape, and the bird is glued on last.

# Basket Arrangements

This *New England Wicker Basket Arrangement* makes a beautiful centerpiece.

Begin by cutting a piece of floral foam to fit the bottom of the basket and securing it with wire. Cover the foam with moss using greening pins and insert the flowers by their stems into the moss.

The dried flowers include: pepper grass, white yarrow, teasel, oak leaf hydrangea, nigella pods, and amaranthus.

This *Swimming Duck Basket* creates a natural-looking habitat for a decoy duck.

The arrangement begins by hot-gluing a cube of floral foam to the bottom of a handleless basket. The decoy is then hot-glued to the foam, with its head arranged to reach over the basket. The water foliage is made from dried grasses, tree fern, palmetto blades, lotus pods, and roses, all arranged to appear to be growing naturally.

# Basket Arrangements

This *Flowering Basket* forms a planter for both fresh and dried materials, and easily decorates a porch, patio, deck, or doorway.

The living plant on the right, a calamander, is placed in the basket inside a pot. The dried bouquet to the left, made from dill, sweet Annie, yarrow, zinnia, berries, tansy, feverfew, ambrosia, princess pine, baby's breath, and German statice, is inserted into a block of floral foam inside the basket.

The floral foam, the pot, and any bare areas are covered with ground moss and then decorated with pine cones. The moss can be lifted when you need to water the plant or rearrange your dried flower bouquet.

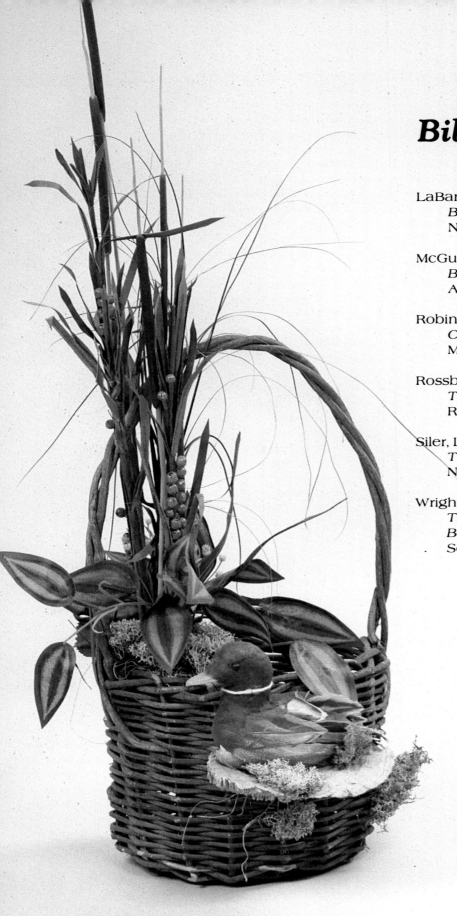

# Bibliography

LaBarge, Lura
    *Basketmaking From The Beginning.*
    New York: Funk & Wagnalls, 1976.

McGuire, John
    *Basketry: The Shaker Tradition.*
    Asheville, North Carolina: Lark Books, 1988.

Robinson, Sharon
    *Contemporary Basketry.* Worcester,
    Massachusetts: Davis Publishing, Inc., 1978.

Rossback, Ed
    *The New Basketry.* New York: Van Nostrand
    Reinhold Company, 1976.

Siler, Lyn
    *The Basket Book.* New York /Asheville,
    North Carolina: Sterling /Lark, 1988.

Wright, Dorothy
    *The Complete Book of Baskets and
    Basketry.* New York: Charles Scribner's
    Sons, 1977.

# Acknowledgements

## Contributing Designers . . .

**Julianne Bronder** (pages 17, 21, 34, 53, 54, 56-right and left, 60-bottom right, 61, 62-top right; 74-top, 76-top, 77, 90-top, 94, 97, 101, 102, 103-top, 106-bottom, 107-top, 110, 111, 112, 113, 114, 115, 123, 124-bottom, 126) is a floral artist and instructor who specializes in innovative and custom design. She makes her home in Asheville, North Carolina.

**Ron Clemmer** (pages 56, 67, 71, 73, 74-bottom, 92, 93) enjoys transforming antique baskets into decorative centerpieces. His store, Fireside Antiques and Interiors, in Asheville, North Carolina, specializes in interior and floral design. All of the freeze-dried materials in his baskets courtesy of Preservations by Kent, Charlotte, North Carolina.

**Cynthia Gillooly** (pages 30-31, 33, 35, 49, 50, 66, 84, 89-top and bottom, 90-bottom) owns the Golden Cricket in Asheville, North Carolina. She specializes in creative, natural design.

**Jeanette Hafner** (pages 62-left, 78-79) has been drying flowers for 30 years and takes pride in growing most of the flowers used to decorate her baskets.

**Nicole Victoria** (pages 32, 40, 44, 47, 48, 64-65, 80, 81, 82, 83, 86, 87-top) owns and operates Nicole's Cottage in Asheville, North Carolina. Nicole also produces a national wholesale line called the "French Victorian Romance Collection."

**Hanford's, Inc.,** of Charlotte, North Carolina, is a national importer and wholesaler of gift lines. Several members of their design team contributed to this book.

**Fred Tyson Gaylor** (pages 60-top left, 87-bottom, 91, 98-top and bottom, 120-right, 122) taught art in the community college system of North Carolina for ten years before becoming involved in designing showroom and movie displays. Fred was also a contributing designer for *The Wreath Book*.

**Michael Monroe** (pages 52, 100, 119) was educated in horticulture and design, and enjoys creating landscape designs in natural settings.

**Anthea Masters** (pages 118, 120-left, 121-right) has enjoyed doing freelance display work for 12 years. Anthea has a particular fondness for antique baskets and old fashioned English garden flowers.

Special thanks also to Hanford designers **Carla Church** (pages 72-bottom, 88), **Scott York** (pages 59, 63), and **Shelby Wirt** (page 41).

## Also Thanks To . . .

Elizabeth Albrecht (pages 20, 68-69, 104)
Bob Gillooly (page 75)
Carol H. Heller (page 46)
Missy Henson (page 88)
Jeanne Pulleyn (pages 39, 103-bottom)
Micah Pulleyn (page 76-bottom)
Rob Pulleyn (pages 72-top, 105-top and bottom)
David Robertson (pages 38, 40, 58)
Betsy Silver (page 99)
Tommy Wolff (pages 55, 84)
Margaret Davidson (pages 6-9, 12-13) Grass Script Company, Seattle, Washington

Michelle Bellamy (page 70) The Chocolate Fetish, Asheville, North Carolina
Earth Guild (pages 10-11) Asheville, North Carolina
Jo-Belle's Craft Supply (page 95) Swannanoa, North Carolina
Little Yellow Flower Farm (pages 96, 106-top, 107-bottom) Leicester, North Carolina
Gail Martin (pages 20-top, 36, 37, 125) Celebrations, Asheville, North Carolina
Nancy McCauley (pages 108, 109, 116, 124-top) Canvas Patch Originals, Oak Ridge, Tennessee
Sandy Mush Herb Nursery (pages 42-43, 45) Leicester, North Carolina

# Index

# Basket Care and Conservation

However sturdy they may look, baskets are made from delicate materials and need attentive care. Some tips to remember:

- Keep baskets away from direct sunlight and intense artificial light to avoid fading, bleaching, and embrittlement.

- Baskets kept near open windows may be damaged by insects or dirt.

- Basketry materials tend to absorb grease, soot, and odors, so choose kitchen locations for baskets with care.

- Realize that placing a basket in a location that frequently experiences drastic temperature or humidity changes (such as bathrooms or walls warmed by a fireplace) will accelerate the basket's aging process.

- Organic basketry materials absorb spills easily.

- Brush dirt and dust from your basket on a regular basis with a soft brush.

- Water and cleaning solvents are affective in cleaning some baskets, but they can also damage or discolor a basket, and there's no way to know until after the deed is done.